KNOW
THEGAME

etta

Table Tennis

Produced in collaboration with the
English Table Tennis Association Ltd

A&
CB

2006 000471

Produced for A & C Black by

Monkey Puzzle Media Ltd
Gissings Farm, Fressingfield
Suffolk IP21 5SH

Published in 2006 by

A & C Black Publishers Ltd
38 Soho Square, London W1D 3HB
www.acblack.com

Fourth edition 2006

ISBN-10: 0 7136 7899 2
ISBN-13: 978 0 7136 7899 4

Note: While every effort has been made to ensure
that the content of this book is as technically accurate
and as sound as possible, neither the author nor the
publisher can accept responsibility for any injury or
loss sustained as a result of the use of this material.

A & C Black uses paper produced with elemental
chlorine-free pulp, harvested from managed
sustainable forests.

Acknowledgements
Cover and inside design by James Winrow for
Monkey Puzzle Media Ltd
Cover photograph courtesy of Empics.
Photographs on pages 47, 48, 49 and 51 courtesy
of Empics. All other photographs throughout the
book courtesy of David Wearn.
Illustrations by Dave Saunders
Many thanks to Ron Crayden for supplying historical
and biographical information, and to Rob Sinclair for
all his help.

KNOW THE GAME is a registered trademark.

Printed and bound in China by C&C Offset Printing
Co. Ltd.

Note: Throughout the book players and officials are
referred to as 'he'. This should, of course, be taken
to mean 'he or she' where appropriate. Similarly, all
instructions are geared towards right-handed players
– left-handers should simply reverse these instructions.

CONTENTS

INTRODUCTION

Table tennis is the biggest racket sport in the world. It can be enjoyed by men and women, and boys and girls of all ages and abilities. It can also be played and enjoyed by those with special needs.

ALL LEVELS AND ABILITIES

Table tennis can be played casually as a relaxing and healthy recreation. It can also be played as a fast-moving and exciting competitive sport. At the top echelons of the game, players are superb athletes with lightning reactions who can propel the ball as fast as 160km/h (100 mph).

EQUIPMENT

The table
Table tennis tables are 2.74m long by 1.525m wide (9 ft x 5 ft) and have a surface thickness of 22–25mm (0.8-0.98 in). The table stands 76cm (2 ft 6 in) above the floor. Smaller mini-tables are available. The main types of full table are:

- standard – with two separate halves

- rollaway – the two halves are mounted on a central undercarriage which has wheels for easy manoeuvrability

- rollaway with playback – a rollaway where one half may be vertical while the other half is horizontal. This allows for one player to practise alone.

Tables are the most expensive item of equipment and should be well cared for. Tables should be stored 'face to face' to prevent the surface from being scratched. They should be stored on the central edge of the two halves since damage to this edge will not affect play.

Player watches the ball carefully during the service action.

AN OLYMPIC SPORT

Table tennis began in the 19th century. In 1926, five nations: Germany, England, Austria, Sweden and Hungary, formed the International Table Tennis Federation which runs the sport today. In 1988, table tennis made its debut at the Seoul Olympics in South Korea. There are four medal events – the men's singles and team and the women's singles and team competitions. The International Olympic Committee estimates that there are over 40 million competitive players throughout the world.

The net and posts

The top of the net is 15.25cm (6 in) above the playing surface. The net posts clamp to the playing top so that the net is held firmly in place. The net usually has a cord through its top so that the net tension can be adjusted. Most nets and posts can be removed from the table for easy storage.

The ball

Balls are made of celluloid or plastic, and are white or orange in colour. The ball is 40mm (1.57 in) in diameter and weigh just 2.7g (0.09 oz). The quality of the ball is determined by a 'star' rating – the higher the rating, the higher the quality. All official competitions are played with three-star celluloid balls.

The table's dimensions and markings.

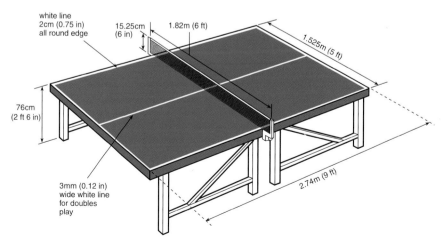

white line
2cm (0.75 in)
all round edge

15.25cm
(6 in)

1.82m (6 ft)

1.525m (5 ft)

76cm
(2 ft 6 in)

3mm (0.12 in)
wide white line
for doubles
play

2.74m (9 ft)

THE RACKET

Table tennis rackets (sometimes called racquets) may be of any size, shape or weight. They are made of a wooden blade, normally covered on each side with a layer known as a rubber. Penhold players (see pages 12–13) may use a racket with rubber on only one side of the blade.

The racket

The blades are made from several layers (or ply) of wood. The number of ply and the softness or hardness of the wood affects the speed and control of the blade. Slow blades are made of three-ply soft wood, whereas very fast blades may be seven-ply with additional layers of carbon fibre. Greater speed generally means less control.

The rubbers have a smooth side and a pimpled side. Most racket rubbers use reversed pimples with the smooth side facing out. Some players, however, use combination rackets, with different rubbers on each side of the blade.

Rubbers must be red on one side of the blade and black on the other side. In the case of a penhold player where only one sheet of rubber is used, the racket must still be red on one side and black on the other. This is usually achieved by staining the blade.

> For beginners, a five-ply all-round racket is recommended. It should have 1.5mm (0.06 in) thick rubbers. This will give you good control and reasonable spin.

 Player moves in, keeping the body low to push return a short ball.

Clothing

Table tennis is a fast, athletic game and clothing should be comfortable and not restrict movement. Short-sleeved shirts and shorts are normally worn. Socks may be any colour but most players wear white. Playing shoes should have a good grip but must be light and flexible for the fast movements that are required. The shoes should support the heel and instep of your foot.

Lighting

Local conditions will vary considerably, but good lighting that is even is important in table tennis. Tungsten halogen lights (minimum 500 Lux) give the best lighting conditions. Ideally, lights should be mounted about 4m (13 ft) high from the floor.

A RUBBER'S THICKNESS

Most rubbers are used with a layer of sponge which is sandwiched between the runner and the wooden blade. The sponge may be between 1.0mm and 2.5mm (0.04 in and 0.1 in) thick. The total thickness of the covering (the rubber and sponge together) on one side must not be more than 4mm (0.16 in).

Table tennis action can be fast and furious. A player's clothing should be comfortable and sweat-absorbent.

BASICS OF TABLE TENNIS

Table tennis is a simple game based on a small number of key rules which can be learned quickly. At the heart of the game is its simple and straightforward scoring system.

This player strives to reach a dipping ball before it hits the floor otherwise they will lose the point.

AIM OF THE GAME

Table tennis involves one or two players per team. They stand behind either end of the table and have to play the ball over the net so that it lands on their opponent's side of the table. The ball is only allowed to bounce once per side of the table. A point begins with one player serving the ball by releasing it from their hand and hitting it with their racket. The ball must bounce on their side of the table first before travelling over the net and bouncing on their opponent's side. The returning player must hit the ball so that it first lands on the opponent's side of the table. A ball cannot be hit on the volley – i.e. before it has bounced on that player's side of the table. This rally continues until an action occurs (see below) which involves a point being scored by one side, such as missing the ball completely or letting the ball bounce twice on one side of the table. The next point begins with the next serve.

SCORING

In table tennis the scoring system is very simple. Either player or pair may score a point, regardless of which player serves. A point is scored if an opponent:

- fails to make a good service or return
- intercepts the ball before it has bounced when it is above or moving towards the playing surface
- hits the ball twice or lets it bounce twice before hitting it
- moves the table or touches it with his free hand
- touches the net
- in doubles, hits the ball out of turn.

Except when the ball is served, it makes no difference whether the ball touches the net as it passes over or around the net.

NUMBER OF SERVES

The number of serves each player gets has varied over the years. An earlier system saw players each take five serves in a row before the serve switched to their opponent. Today, each player or each pair in a doubles match serve for 2 points in a row before the serve switches. The one exception is when the score in a game reaches 10-10. In this case, players or teams serve once before swapping serve.

A player has to let the ball bounce once on their side before hitting it back to their opponent's court.

WINNING A GAME

A game is won by the first player or pair to score 11 points, unless both have scored 10 points. When the score is 10-10, the winner is the first player or pair to gain a lead of 2 points – for example, 12-10 or 15-13. A match can be the best of any odd number of games, but it is usually 5 or 7 games.

DOUBLES RULES

The rules for doubles games are a little more complicated. In doubles, the players must hit the ball alternately and in a strict order known as rotation. This means that during a game, a player always receives the ball from the same opponent and hits the ball to the other opponent. The serving player, A, must hit the ball to either opponent X or Y who must then play to the server's partner, B. This means that there are only 2 possible orders of play: A, X, B, Y, A; or A, Y, B, X, A.

If A serves to opponent X in the first game, in the second game either X must serve to A or Y must serve to B. In the third game, A must serve to X or B serve to Y, and so on. In the deciding game, the order is reversed as soon as either pair scores 5 points.

 Doubles partners celebrate after winning a match.

THE EXPEDITE SYSTEM

Just like the tie-break in tennis, the expedite system was introduced to prevent unduly long games. It is designed to encourage the server to attack and to produce exciting, entertaining play. The system is introduced after 10 minutes of play (or at any time earlier if both players or pairs agree). Once the system has been introduced, it remains in force for the remainder of the match.

Under this system, the players serve only one service each in turn. The server then has 12 strokes after his service to win the point. If his service and the 12 subsequent strokes are safely returned by the receiver, then the receiver wins the point. The game is won in the normal way by a player winning 11 points, or after 10-all by two clear points.

A doubles match at the point where one player is about to serve to another.

CHOOSING SERVE

In each game, the pair with the right to serve first can choose which of them will do so. In the first game the receiving pair can then choose which of them will receive first and in which subsequent game the sequence must be reversed.

When playing doubles, keep focused on who you're receiving from and playing to otherwise you could lose points cheaply.

BASIC SKILLS

New players need to learn the game's basic skills and practice them as often as they can. The basic skills consist of the grip, striking the ball correctly and at the right angle and putting spin on the ball.

THE GRIP

The grip controls the angle of the racket, which in turn influences the ball in many ways:

- the height the ball travels at
- the depth that the ball reaches
- the speed at which the ball will travel
- the type of spin
- the amount of spin
- the degree of 'touch' – power and speed of the racket at the contact point.

> **Keep the three fingers on the handle of the racket as loose as possible to reduce muscle tension and give you the maximum degree of touch.**

Shake-hands grip

The shake-hands grip is like saying 'hello' to the racket. The thumb and forefinger lay on the blade of the racket, with the three remaining fingers loosely around the handle in the palm of the hand. It is the most common type of grip used by players in open play.

The shake-hands grip sees the player's forefinger steady the racket at the back.

Penhold grip

The 'penhold' grip is popular in Asian countries. There are two forms: Chinese and Japanese. It is called 'penhold' because you hold the racket just like you would grip a pen. However, only one side of the racket is used, which some players find limiting.

MAKING ADJUSTMENTS

Table tennis calls on players to adapt constantly as every ball that approaches them has a different direction, spin, speed and path or trajectory. One of the most important skills required by a player is perception – the ability to judge the type of shot arriving to them – so that they can adjust:

- the angle of their racket
- the angle of their swing
- the degree of touch.

RACKET ANGLES

An open racket angle is when the racket is sloping backwards when striking the ball. A closed angle is when the racket is sloping forwards. An open angle will neutralise an approaching ball which has backspin (see overleaf). A closed angle used with a fast-moving swing in an upward direction will increase the spin on the ball.

A closed angle of racket will neutralise an approaching ball which has been hit with topspin. An open angle racket moving fast downwards will increase the spin on the ball with the ball still rotating on the same axis.

 The penhold grip sees the racket angled downwards and the player's thumb and forefinger meeting at the base of the handle.

Open and closed racket angles.

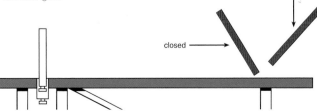

open

closed

STRIKING POINT

Where possible, the striking point of the ball should be made at about chest height and at an equal distance from each shoulder. It helps a player's strokes, accuracy and rhythm if the ball is hit at the same striking point each time.

SPIN

Players need to learn how to put different types of spin on the ball. Large amounts of spin can be really effective when serving. The ball is generally struck with either topspin or backspin. If there is little or no spin on the ball, it is referred to as 'float'.

Topspin
Topspin is produced by starting the stroke below and/or behind the ball, and contacting the ball as lightly as possible, i.e. brushing the ball in an upward and forward motion.

Backspin
Backspin is produced by starting the stroke above and/or behind the ball and contacting the ball as lightly as possible, i.e. brushing the ball in a downward and/or forward motion.

CONTACT POINTS

By picturing the ball as a clock face, we can comprehend the simplest example of spin. Contacting the ball with a brushing action of:

- 2–12 in an upward direction = topspin
- 4–6 in a downwards direction = backspin
- 3 or 9 in a sideways direction (going round the side of the ball) = sidespin

On the diagram:
T = topspin
B = backspin

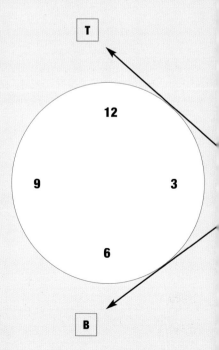

Sidespin

Sidespin is produced by brushing across the ball lightly. This spin can be added to the ball at the same time as either topspin or backspin.

Hitting the ball at 3 or 9 o'clock, going around the side of the ball, gives sidespin.

Hitting the ball with the racket moving to the right adds spin so that when it lands, the ball will move to the right.

Hitting while the racket moves to the left will spin the ball to the left when it lands.

> **When striking the ball, use your free hand to point and trace the ball. Strike the ball when it is adjacent to your free hand.**

▼ The ball is thrown up straight and contact will be made using an accelerating racket as the ball drops.

DEVELOPING SKILLS

After mastering the basic skills such as the grip, players need to develop key skills involving positioning, timing, learning to read the ball, control it and using the correct racket angle and action to strike it.

PERCEPTION

Players must learn to adopt a good ready position. This is the posture and position which players should both start in before they make a stroke and finish in after they have completed their stroke. Your feet should be shoulder-width apart with the knees flexed. Your bodyweight should be balanced evenly so that you are able to move quickly in any direction. It also helps if you stay on your toes and balls of your feet.

Your exact position relative to the edge of the table depends on the target area the player selects (see the diagrams).

▼ A player in a good ready position is able to react to most of their opponent's shots.

Reading the play

Learning to read the play in a game only comes with lots of practice and match experience. It involves keeping your eyes on the game with full concentration at all times. To read the play, you obviously have to watch the ball. But you also have to watch your opponent before and as they strike the ball in order to pick up clues as to what sort of shot they are playing and where the ball is likely to head. Players should watch and note the following actions of their opponent:

- their body position and movement
- the speed and direction of their swing
- the angle of their racket.

Reading the play is only effective if the player has the speed and reactions to exploit their assessment of the play by moving into a good position to make their reply.

An extremely effective tip is to use your free hand as a sort of radar system, tracking the ball and its flight during the rally.

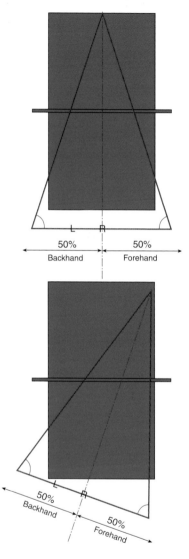

The ready position varies depending on the target area selected by the player. In all cases, though, the player should try to position themselves so that they cover as much of the table with their backhand and forehand sides.

DECISIONS

Players have a large range of decisions they have to make every shot. These include the choice of stroke and the amount of spin and power to attempt to put on the ball as well as the exact target area they are aiming for the ball to hit on their opponent's side of the table.

Key decisions involve a player's timing, table position and base movement.

- Timing – try to hit the ball at its highest point, as this will allow you to play the ball downwards in a straight line over the net to your intended target (see bottom diagram opposite).

- Table position – try to hit the ball as early as possible and in front of you to find the widest angles with the greatest degree of accuracy (see top diagram opposite).

- Base movement – move from the ready position using the nearest foot to the ball to a position slightly behind the contact point between racket and ball.

After each stroke, return to a neutral position with the racket in front of you and over the table. This will make playing your next stroke easier.

Player keeps his bodyweight low and turns his shoulder to reach a very short ball.

ACTION

- Body action – try to keep the centre of gravity of your body low and at a constant height. Lean from one foot to the other to transfer your weight for strokes.

- Racket arm – use the shoulder joint for power strokes, the elbow for maximum control and the wrist for speed/spin strokes.

- Try to make sure that around half of the forward movement of the racket occurs before contact with the ball. This helps ensure that you have good racket speed as you meet the ball.

See how hitting the ball earlier and closer to the table gives a player a greater chance of hitting a wide angle, making it difficult for their opponent to return the ball.

This shows the ideal timing point for striking a ball at its highest point after it has bounced on your end of the table.

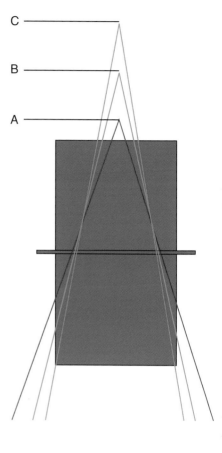

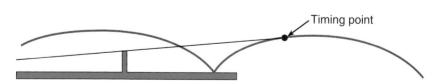

Timing point

TACTICAL STROKE PLAY

Tactical stroke play involves a small selection of basic shots which players may find they use a great deal during a game. They include backhand and forehand pushes and drives.

FOREHAND AND BACKHAND PUSH STROKES

Both push strokes see the ball travel and land with backspin. The shots share similarities in how you approach and play them.

Perception
- Adopt a ready position in relation to your last target and facing the ball.
- Watch your opponent's actions carefully and track the ball with the free hand.

Decisions
- Try to strike the ball at its highest spot, as near to the table as comfortable and moving the nearest foot to the ball.

Action
- Staying in a low posture, strike using an elbow action with 50% of the forward movement of the racket before contact.

Player uses an open bat to produce a forehand push to return a short ball.

BACKHAND PUSH

Backhand push strokes are very effective when you are unable to attack the ball. The stroke is made from the ready position with your knees bent and standing on the balls of your feet. The stroke begins with your elbow bent upward and the racket held up near the chest, level in an open angle. Pivot your elbow downward and push through the ball, making sure you don't slap or jerk the ball. By stroking the back of the ball and underneath it, you aim to send it back low and slow over the net onto the receiver's side of the table.

AIM FOR THE BASELINE

A good push shot is a stroke that lands the ball as close to your opponent's baseline as possible. This will make it difficult for your opponent to attack with power and depth, making it easier for you to attack on your next stroke.

FOREHAND PUSHING

The forehand push involves a similar racket angle and stroke as the backhand push but is on the forehand side. The stroke starts with your upper body turning back slightly, keeping your elbow close to your hip. The forward swing of the racket should aim to meet the ball at the top of its bounce. Pivot the elbow down and stroke under the ball in the same way as the backhand push.

> **Keep the three fingers on the racket handle loose when playing push shots.**

Player uses the backhand block to counter the opponent's speed.

FOREHAND AND BACKHAND TOPSPIN DRIVING

Driving strokes are powerful strokes used to attack your opponent. Good driving shots produce travel low over the net with topspin on the ball. They are used to force errors from your opponent and also to set up your own winning shots. With both strokes, it is important to strike the ball early with speed, aiming for a target that is deep and/or angled. This will help reduce your opponent's organisation time and potentially increase your own time if your opponent drops back. Use this stroke when the approaching ball has height and/or depth.

When attacking against backspin, the movement of your topspin stroke should be upward and with a slightly more 'open' racket. When attacking against a topspin ball, the movement of the stroke is more forward, with a more 'closed' racket.

The movement of your stroke in topspin drives is similar to the movement you would use to throw a flying disc.

Perception
- Adopt a ready position in relation to your last target and facing the ball.
- Watch your opponent's actions carefully and track the ball with the free hand.

Decisions
- Try to strike the ball at the highest point, as near to the table as comfortable, having moved the nearest foot towards the ball. Aim to make contact with the ball ahead of your body.

Action
- Staying in a low posture, strike using a slight but fast rotation of the upper body on forehand strokes, with a shoulder action, with 50% of the forward movement of the racket before contact.

 A young player learning to play a forehand drive.

With backhand topspin drives, the upper body rotates only slightly but the legs stay facing the line of play.

ADVANCED STROKES

Once drives and pushes are mastered, players should move on to more advanced strokes. A player with a wide range of shots in their armoury will have more options to win points during a game.

THE BLOCK – FOREHAND OR BACKHAND

The block is a very short stroke, generally played without spin. It is taken very early and hit deep and sometimes at an angle. It is used to reduce the organisation time of the opponent and/or to neutralise the spin on the ball. You are in a situation where you do not have time to generate speed or spin and would still choose to keep your opponent under pressure.

Technique – forehand block

The racket is drawn back towards the left hip in a slightly closed position. On the forward swing the forearm moves forward and slightly upward with the racket angle slightly closed according to the amount of spin on the ball. More spin, more closed.

 The player tries to recover from being out of position.

Technique – backhand block

Use a short backswing with the racket slightly closed and the elbow forming a 90° angle. The racket arm moves forward and upward from the elbow and the racket angle is slightly closed according to the amount of spin on the ball.

Perception

- Adopt a ready position in relation to your last target and facing the ball.
- Watch your opponent's actions carefully and track the ball with the free hand.

Decisions

- Try to strike the ball as early as possible and as near to the table as comfortable, having moved the nearest foot towards the ball.

Action

- Stay in a low, crouched position and use as little approach to the ball as possible while striking with a loose wrist action.

Strike the ball as early as possible with the fingers on the handle of the racket as loose as possible and with a relaxed wrist.

 This player's eye is focused firmly on the ball during service.

FOREHAND AND BACKHAND LOOP

The forehand and backhand loop strokes are variations of the topspin drives (see pages 22–23). Strike the ball with as much topspin to a target that is deep and/or angled. This will reduce your opponent's ability to control the ball and will potentially increase your chances of a high return. Use this stroke when the approaching ball is only just high or long enough to attack, or when the approaching ball has excessive backspin.

Technique – forehand loop

The racket arm moves backwards and downwards lower than the height of the ball. The hips, waist and shoulders rotate the weight on to the right leg. On the forward movement the racket moves upwards as the legs straighten and the hips, waist and shoulders unwind. The forearm accelerates and the racket brushes the ball soon after peak bounce.

 Player reacts to a ball played fast with a crossover step.

Technique – backhand loop

The racket arm moves backwards and downwards to just outside the left hip below the height of the ball. There is a slight rotation to the left at the waist. The racket arm moves upwards and forwards from the elbow as the waist unwinds.
The forearm accelerates and the racket brushes the ball soon after peak bounce.

> **Create as much racket speed as possible, but with only a light degree of touch brushing against the ball. This often means that the ball will travel slowly but have extreme spin.**

Perception

- Adopt a ready position in relation to your last target and facing the ball.

- Watch your opponent's actions carefully and track the ball with the free hand.

Decisions

- Try to strike the ball as early as possible and as near to the table as comfortable, having moved the nearest foot towards the ball. Keep your grip loose.

Action

- Staying in a low posture, strike using a slight but fast rotation of the upper body with a shoulder, elbow action with 50% of the forward movement of the racket before contact.

A young player shows his concentration and follow through after playing a forehand topspin.

FOREHAND AND BACKHAND CHOP

The chop is the main weapon of a defensive player. It is mostly played well back from the table with backspin and contact as the ball is dropping. The distance away from the table is thus determined by the speed of the attacking shot. Defensive players change the contact point on the ball to produce varying degrees of spin, ranging from heavy backspin to no spin.

Strike the ball early with speed and topspin to a target that is deep and/or angled. This will reduce your opponent's organisation time and potentially increase your own time if your opponent drops back. Use this stroke when the approaching ball has height and/or depth.

Technique – forehand chop

In preparation to make the stroke the right leg moves back as the elbow is bent and the racket is brought backwards and upwards to head height. With the forward swing the forearm and wrist move forwards and downwards brushing the bottom part of the ball with a slightly open racket angle.

Technique – backhand chop

In preparation, the left leg moves back, the elbow is bent, and the racket is brought backwards and upwards to shoulder height. With the forward swing, the forearm and wrist move forwards and downwards, brushing the bottom of the ball with a slightly open racket angle.

Perception

- Adopt a ready position in relation to your last target and facing the ball.

- Watch your opponent's actions carefully and track the ball with the free hand.

Decisions

- Try to strike the ball at a high spot, as near to the table as comfortable.

Action

- Staying in a low posture, strike the ball using an elbow action with 50% of the forward movement of the racket before contact.

Always strike the ball as early as possible for maximum effect.

This sequence shows the preparation, contact and follow through of the forehand chop shot.

SERVICE AND RETURN

Good, varied serving and excellent returning of serve are keys to table tennis success. Top players use a wide range of services, trying to disguise as much as possible the type of spin, the amount of spin, and the speed and direction of the ball.

SERVING

To serve, the ball must be thrown upwards without spin from the open palm of the server's hand. The ball must rise at least 16cm (6.3 in). It should be struck when it is falling from the highest point of its flight. It must be struck so that it bounces on the server's half of the table, passes over or around the net, and then bounces on the receiver's side of the table. If in service the ball touches the net but the service is otherwise correct, the umpire calls a let; no point is scored and the service is taken again.

From the start of service until it is struck, the ball:

- must be behind the server's end line
- above the level of the playing surface
- must not be hidden from the receiver by any part of the body or clothing of the server or of the server's doubles partner.

Player's body is low and racket is in position to start the service action when the ball has been thrown up.

The ball is in play from the time at which it leaves the server's hand. This means that once it has been thrown, a miss or a poor throw will mean that the opponent scores a point. However, if the ball is accidentally dropped before it is thrown, no point is scored because the ball was not in play.

After the ball has been correctly served, play continues until one player fails to make a good return and so loses the point.

When serving, use a loose grip to increase the range of your wrist movement.

SWITCHING SIDES

Advanced players often use forehand services from the backhand side of the table. This allows the players to use different angles of play and increase the opportunity to follow up their serve with a very strong forehand topspin loop stroke. The player requires rapid footwork for this to work well as the whole table has to be covered with the forehand.

Player reacts quickly to play a forehand topspin.

SERVE OR RECEIVE?

The first server in a match is decided by the toss of a coin. The winner of the toss can choose to serve or receive first, or to start play at a particular end of the table. If the winner decides to serve or receive, the loser can choose the end, and vice versa. The players change ends after every game, and again in the deciding game, when first one player or pair scores 5 points.

A serving pair in a doubles match, with one player about to serve and the other in the ready position to play the team's next shot.

A good return can pass over the net at any point in its length. Remember, that a good return can also pass around the side of or under the net post.

Doubles

In doubles, each court is divided into halves by a white centre line. The ball has to bounce diagonally from the right-hand half of the server's court to the right-hand half of the receiver's court. The centre line is regarded as part of each right-hand half-court, so the service is good if the ball bounces on it.

A young player uses good timing to execute his return using a forehand drive.

RETURNING SERVICE

The player receiving the service should be in a ready position. They must be able to move easily in any direction to cover every possible angle that the server may use. The stroke used to return service depends on the type of serve, but generally, forehand and backhand topspin drives are used to return topspin and long serves, while forehand and backhand pushes are used for short serves with backspin.

A good return is when the ball bounces once only on the receiver's half of the table. It must then be hit (a 'hit' includes the hand holding the racket) and returned to the opponent's side without touching any obstacle other than the net. There is no height limit to the path of the ball. It may pass above the lights but it must not touch them. If the ball touches any obstacle the ball is 'dead' and the last striker loses the point.

A player is allowed to follow a spinning ball back across the net and strike it over the opponent's half of the table as long as he does not touch the net or net posts with his racket or clothing.

WARM-UP AND COOL-DOWN

When played competitively, table tennis is a highly athletic sport which uses almost every muscle group in your body. Like any strenuous sport, it is important to warm up and stretch before playing as well as cooling-down afterwards.

WARMING UP

Your warm-up should last 15 to 20 minutes and take place just prior to the beginning of your practice session or match. Warming up raises your heart rate, helping you get ready for the match action ahead. It also helps to warm your body's muscles which not only helps prevent injuries but also gets the joints moving freely. Some players also feel that some physical exertion helps get their minds focused on playing the match as well. Warming up usually consists of some light jogging as well as moves such as skipping or star jumps. All warm-up exercises should start out at a gentle level and gradually increase in intensity.

 Stretching exercise being performed.

STRETCHING

After warming up, a series of muscle stretches should be performed. These help prevent injury and ensure that your body is ready for action. A stretching programme should cover the whole body, starting at the top and working down as follows:

- neck and shoulders (do not roll the neck in a full circle as this may cause damage to the vertebrae)
- arms and chest
- lower back and stomach
- groin and hips
- upper legs
- knees
- lower legs and ankles.

You may be impatient to start your match or training session, but do spend just the few minutes necessary to complete the stretching programme. Concentrate on each stretching exercise. Stretches should be gentle and the stretched position held for a few seconds before being repeated. Ballistic stretching exercises which involve bouncing or jerking movements, could cause injury and should always be avoided.

COOL-DOWN

Cool-downs after a match or extensive training will help to avoid any stiffness or soreness in a player's muscles. Different players have different cool-down routines, but slow jogging or walking and light stretching are ideal. Such gentle exercises should be continued for a few minutes until the body returns to a near resting state.

> **Ask your coach to demonstrate and show you how to perform suitable stretching exercises for all of your key muscle groups.**

Several players performing warming up exercises.

PRACTICE

People play table tennis for different reasons – for fun, as a social occasion, for exercise and for competition. Whatever the level or purpose of playing, all players can benefit from practice to improve their game.

TYPES OF PRACTICE

Whether you play for fun or in competition, winning tends to be more enjoyable than losing. To be successful in table tennis, as in any other sport, players must spend time practising.

Practice can be divided into two main elements:

> 1) Practice that improves the strokes known as technical practice.
>
> 2) Practice that improves a player's tactical awareness and ability. This is known as tactical practice.

TECHNICAL PRACTICE

Technical practice is divided into two types: regular and irregular practice.

Regular practice
This is where both players hit the ball knowing its direction and giving the ball a specific speed and spin. This type of practice is very good for a player's technical development. It gives a player a chance to work on and groove a particular type of stroke so that they can make that shot consistently and with confidence. It also allows players to recognize an opponent's racket actions and the kind of shot they lead to as well as giving them experience of responding to specific shots.

Irregular practice
This is where the player does not know where the opponent's ball is going. This practice helps players learn how to read their opponent's racket angle, the direction and speed of the shot.

Take your practice seriously by warming up and stretching beforehand and concentrating throughout a practice session.

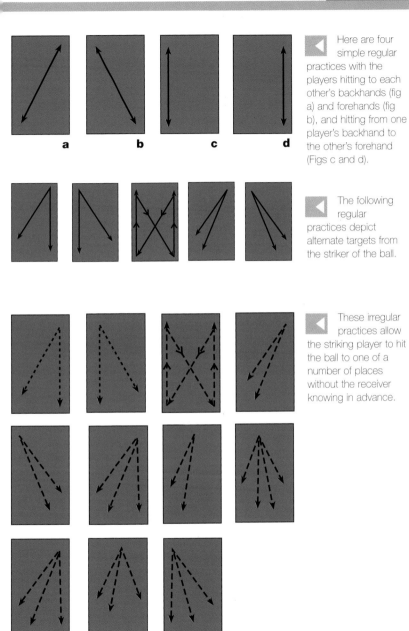

Here are four simple regular practices with the players hitting to each other's backhands (fig a) and forehands (fig b), and hitting from one player's backhand to the other's forehand (Figs c and d).

a   **b**   **c**   **d**

The following regular practices depict alternate targets from the striker of the ball.

These irregular practices allow the striking player to hit the ball to one of a number of places without the receiver knowing in advance.

TACTICAL DEVELOPMENT AND PRACTICE

There are three stages of tactical development:

1. Keeping the ball in play.

2. Developing accuracy with strokes to a large range of target positions on the table.

3. Applying pressure with spin, speed and by striking the ball early to different targets.

There are two types of practice that help develop tactical skills: regular and irregular free practice.

Regular-free practice

This is where the player knows exactly how the ball will be played at them, but only for a set number of strokes. After this it can be placed anywhere. This 'free' element of the practice helps players develop tactical awareness.

Irregular-free practice

In irregular-free practice, the ball is initially placed in a particular area of the court – for example, the forehand court – but can arrive from a variety of shots. Once a certain number of strokes have been played into that area of the court, the practice becomes 'free', as with regular-free practice.

The robot

Practices may include the use of a 'robot'. This is a machine that shoots balls out at pre-set speeds and spins. If used properly, robots are useful aids for improving strokes in showing practice and for a single player if he does not have an available partner.

Multi-ball

Multi-ball practice is also popular. This is when a coach 'feeds' a number of balls in quick succession to a player. This is better than using a robot because the feeder can vary the spin, speed and positioning of the ball (in testing practice) to offer a more realistic practice. It also demands full concentration from the player and is physically very demanding. The English Table Tennis Association (ETTA) skills award scheme lists more practices that are suitable for players of different standards.

ENJOYABLE GAMES

Table tennis can be a lot of fun and there are numerous variations of the main game that can be used to maintain the enjoyment while retaining a competitive element.

Overtaking

The players balance the ball on their rackets and run around the outside of the playing area. Anyone who is overtaken or who drops the ball is out. This can be advanced with players bouncing the ball on their racket using the forehand, backhand or alternating forehand and backhand.

Minute rallies

Two players play a rally and count the number of strokes played in one minute. A variation is to count the number of strokes played without a mistake.

Round the table

All players are at one end of the table with a feeder at the other end. After hitting the ball, each player must run around the table to rejoin the line. A variation of this game is to have equal numbers at each end of the table and the players run to the opposite end after hitting the ball. Players have three lives, one of which is forfeited each time they make a mistake.

Practise consistency, accuracy and applying pressure on your opponent by selecting targets on both the table and your opponent.

▶ A young player learns how to throw the ball up straight and have the racket ready to make a good service.

▼ Players enjoy a game of 'round the table' which can be used as a fun way of ending practice or at its start.

Team singles

This game sees one player from each team playing a point. The losing player is replaced by the next member of his team for the second point and so on. The winning player stays on but if they win three points in a row, they must retire. The first team to 11 points wins that game.

Targets

Here are three games in which players aim at a specific target on the table to help improve the accuracy of their strokes.

- A small target such as a postcard is placed on the table. Two players play a rally on one diagonal and score points as normal. If they hit the ball onto the target they score two points.

- A larger target (e.g. an A3 sheet of paper) is placed on either side of the net. Each player serves alternately, aiming to hit the target. When the target has been hit three times, the paper is cut in half. Each player aims to make his target smaller than his opponent's.

- In teams, players serve to various targets of differing sizes, scoring points if they are successful. Points may be allocated according to each target's difficulty – its size and position.

 Two players in position to play a point in a doubles match.

The player has thrown up the ball and moved his free arm out of the way ready to serve.

Cricket

Each team has a minimum of three players. One team rackets and the other fields. One of the fielding team throws the ball underarm over the net at head height. The ball should bounce on the opposite side of the table. The racketsman hits the ball so that it lands on the opposite side of the table and then onto the floor before the fielders can catch the ball. If successful the racketter scores a run and continues their innings. The racketter is out if they:

• miss the ball

• hit the ball into the net

• miss the table

• are caught out.

When all players on the racketting side have had an innings, the teams change over.

Relays

In teams, the first player runs to the table, makes a legal serve and then runs around the table and catches the ball after it has bounced once and before it hits the floor. If successful, their team scores one point and the player runs to give the ball to the next player. This can be held as a race over adjacent tables, or timed, if only one table is available. The quickest team to score ten points wins.

If the relay game is too hard for a group of players, allow two bounces on the table or even, one bounce on the floor.

PROGRAMME PLANNING

To be successful at competitive table tennis, it is essential that your training programme is well organised and carefully planned.

SESSION PLANNING

A single session might be planned as follows:

- warm-up – 15 minutes
- knock-up (free play against an opponent, but without keeping score) – 10 minutes
- regular training (where you know the placement of the ball) – 15 minutes
- match play (playing a competitive match against another player) – 15 minutes
- cool-down – 5 minutes.

PHYSICAL TRAINING

Physical fitness is vital for successful table tennis. Physical training should include work on a player's speed, strength, flexibility and stamina – the ability to perform work for long periods. The intensity of the physical training will depend on the age and the standard of the players. Casual players may not be interested in physical training, but those players who are aiming to compete at as high a level as possible need excellent all-round fitness.

Some physical training, such as multi-ball drills can be performed on the table. Most stamina and flexibility work is practised off the table. This includes distance running, skipping and a variety of stretching exercises.

Two pairs compete in a doubles match in a sports hall.

PERIODISATION

The serious competitor needs to make long-term plans for their training. This is called periodisation. The aim is to train so that the player 'peaks' for important competitions. A periodised yearly cycle for juniors would include three phases:

- preparation
- competition
- rest.

The preparation phase would be from July to early September. This time is used to concentrate on improving technique and tactical awareness.

In the Northern Hemisphere, the competition phase runs from September to the end of May. This is when players are competing in various competitions and trying to gain the best possible results.

TIMING OF PERIODISATION

The timings of the preparation, competition and rest phases will vary depending on the level of play. For example, the European Youth Championships take place in July and this would be included in the competition phase.

The rest phase is in June when competitions have finished. Players do not stay inactive. Instead, it is a time when they should play other sports to maintain their fitness without getting stale by playing too much table tennis.

▶ Training hard is very important, but players must be careful to rest at certain times of the year.

COACHING

Players who wish to improve their playing standards will need to have some coaching. Many schools run table tennis clubs where there is a member of staff who has some expertise. However, for players wishing to proceed further up the ladder of success, joining a club is the best way forward.

FINDING A CLUB

Lists of local clubs can be found in libraries or by contacting the National Governing Body (see pages 54–55). Once in a club, players will be able to progress through the Coaching Scheme. If they reach national potential, they will be able to attend the National Academy and hopefully play for their country.

ETTA SKILLS AWARD SCHEME

The English Table Tennis Association (ETTA) have produced a skills award scheme which has ten different levels or grades. This scheme offers a programme of practices which are suitable for all levels and abilities of players. The awards are open to all young players and are suitable for people with disabilities. The purpose of the ETTA skills award scheme is to encourage young players to develop their table tennis skills and so want to play the game at a higher level.

There are ten awards:

- Grades 1 and 2 Polyracket – designed for players with disabilities

- Grades 1 to 5 – introductory awards which link in with the Youth Sports Trust TOP Sport Table Tennis. These are designed to excite new players to table tennis

- Grades 1 to 3 Advanced – these awards require correct stroke production and are more challenging for the young player.

The tests for each of these awards are detailed on the following pages.

BUTTERFLY TABLE TENNIS SKILLS PROGRAMME

This is a national youth development programme designed to support teachers, coaches and leaders by offering lesson plans, competition and festival ideas, skill practices and skills awards. The programme resources are designed to introduce young people to table tennis and provide activities to encourage a lifetime involvement in the sport.

The programme includes:

- Butterfly skills awards – a series of inclusive and progress skill tests at Starter, Improver and Advanced levels for all key stages.

- Butterfly skills learning programmes – activities designed mainly for use in schools across Key Stages 2, 3 and 4.

- Butterfly TT skills circuit – 8 activity stations using transferable racket and ball skills to develop hand-eye coordination in a competitive environment. The circuit is suitable for use in pairs or as an inter-school team festival involving up to 64 players (at Key Stage 2 and 3).

Other programmes and resources

The following programmes and resources are also useful for the coaching and playing of table tennis:

- National Coaching Scheme

- Junior Umpire Award

- TT Networker (Table Tennis Leadership Award)

- Junior League Programme

- Table Tennis competition ladder board.

Further information

Further information and award packs can be obtained by contacting the Coaching Administrator at the:

English Table Tennis Association Ltd.
Third Floor, Queensbury House
Havelock Road, Hastings
East Sussex TN34 1HF

Email: coaching@etta.co.uk
Website: www@etta.co.uk

 Young players holding their awards certificates.

POLYRACKET TESTS

Polyracket is an adapted form of table tennis for players with disabilities. It features a flat racket and raised sides of the table known as rebound boards. There are two levels of tests for Polyracket play.

Grade One Polyracket
1. Hit ball over halfway line – forehand x 5.
2. Hit ball over halfway line – backhand x 5.
3. Serve ball over halfway line – forehand x 5.
4. Serve ball over halfway line – backhand x 5.
5. Hit ball – forehand x 5.
6. Hit ball – forehand x 5.
7. Hit moving ball – forehand x 5.
8. Hit moving ball – backhand x 5.

Class A players achieve 5 tasks.
Class B players achieve 6 tasks.
Class C players achieve 7 tasks.
Class D players achieve 8 tasks.

Grade Two Polyracket
1. Hit ball using sides – forehand x 5.
2. Hit ball using sides – backhand x 5.
3. Hit ball to right corner x 5.
4. Hit ball to left corner x 5.
5. Serve ball to right corner x 5.
6. Serve ball to left corner x 5.
7. Return of service – forehand x 5.
8. Return of service – backhand x 5.
9. Forehand rally x 5.
10. Backhand rally x 5.

Class A players achieve 6 tasks.
Class B players achieve 7 tasks.
Class C players achieve 8 tasks.
Class D players achieve 9 tasks.

ASSESSOR NOTES

These tests should be conducted on tables using specialised Polyracket equipment. Assessors should use their discretion when determining the quality of the candidate's playing ability.

INTRODUCTORY TESTS

The five grades of introductory tests in the ETTA skills award scheme call on players to gradually develop their ball control and awareness skills. The players progress from simple ball balances to directed services and short rallies.

Grade One
1. Balance ball on racket and move – forehand.
2. Balance ball on racket and move – backhand.
3. Jog and balance ball on racket.
4. Bounce ball on racket 5 times – forehand.
5. Bounce ball on racket 5 times – backhand.
6. Drop and hit ball over net 5 times – backhand push.

Grade two
1. Move and bounce ball on racket – forehand.
2. Move and bounce ball on racket – backhand.
3. Drop and hit ball over net 5 times – forehand drive.
4. Hit moving ball over net x 5 – backhand push.
5. Backhand push rally x 5.
6. Basic service – forehand or backhand x 3.

Grade Three
1. Move quickly and bounce ball on racket – forehand.
2. Move quickly and bounce ball on racket – backhand.
3. Alternate bouncing on racket x 5.
4. Hit moving ball over net x 5 – forehand drive.
5. Forehand drive rally x 5.
6. Legal service x 3.

Grade Four
1. Drop and hit ball over net – backhand drive x 5.
2. Backhand drive rally x 5.
3. Backhand drive and forehand drive rally x 6.
4. Forehand drive with movement x 6.
5. Forehand drive controlling direction x 6.
6. Service – 3 forehand, 3 backhand.

Grade Five

1. Backhand drive and forehand drive with movement.
2. Backhand drive controlling direction.
3. Forehand drive controlling direction.
4. Service length – 3 short and 3 long (backhand and forehand).
5. Service direction – 3 line and 3 diagonal (backhand and forehand).
6. Smash x 3.

Assessor notes

Candidates should be able to hold the racket with the correct grip when performing each of the strokes described.

ADVANCED TESTS

Grade One Advanced
1. Backhand push rally x 30.
2. Forehand drive rally x 30.
3. Backhand drive rally x 30.
4. Forehand push rally x 15.
5. Service x 10.
6. Return of service x 10 – short and long, backhand and forehand.

Grade Two Advanced
1. Combined forehand and backhand drive V x 30.
2. Control of forehand and backhand drive V x 30.
3. Combined forehand and backhand push H x 30.
4. Combined forehand and backhand push X x 30.
5. Service variation x 10.
6. Return of varied services x 10.

Key to strokes:

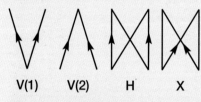

V(1)   V(2)   H   X

Grade Three Advanced
1. Alternate topspin and backspin x 10 – forehand and backhand.
2. Alternate topspin and push x 10 – forehand and backhand.
3. Backhand to backhand topspin and then smash x 5.
4. Advanced serve (pendulum) x 10.
5. Third ball attack x 5.
6. Game situation – tactical awareness.

Assessor notes
Candidates attempting the advanced tests should show good stroke production and consistency of play.

COACHING DISABLED PLAYERS

The basic principles and techniques used when coaching and working with disabled players are the same as those used with non-disabled players. The major area that coaches need to concentrate on is that of communication.

Deaf and hearing-impaired players
- When talking to players, remember always to face the person you are speaking to.
- Speak normally, even when a person is lip reading.
- Do not shout.
- Demonstrate shots and techniques.
- If necessary, write down information.

Blind and visually-impaired players
- Experiment with the size and colour of the balls used.
- Ensure the playing area is clear of any obstacles.
- Allow players time to orientate themselves in the hall and playing areas.
- Do not move equipment without informing the players.
- Do not walk away from players without telling them.

Learning disability

- Give out information in small pieces.

- Be prepared to go over and repeat instructions and information.

- Be patient.

- Keep checking for understanding.

- Treat players according to their age.

- Always speak to the player, but if unsure, check with the parent or carer.

Standing physical impairment

With standing players, there is no real difference in communication. However, one should take into account a player's mobility and whether they need to use crutches or sticks.

Wheelchair users

- Check whether the wheelchair is suitable for physical activity and if the player is able to hold their body erect. Coaches may try removing arm rests to allow additional movement but always ask the player first.

- For beginners it is normally appropriate to play with the brakes on, but as they progress they can experiment playing with the brakes off – if the player feels confident.

- When talking to a wheelchair user for any length of time, sit or kneel to make it more comfortable for the player.

- Do not lean on the wheelchair, as this is part of the player's personal space.

HEALTH AND SAFETY

Remember that you are required by law to deliver a greater duty of care when working with disabled people.

Ensure that the table tennis table does not have a bar across its end underneath the table. If it does it should be at least 40cm (16 in) from the end of the table. If it is less than this amount, one option is to cover the bar with foam rubber so that if wheelchair players hit it with their legs, there is some protection.

If the fire alarm sounds, ensure any deaf or hearing-impaired people are made aware. If required to evacuate, ensure any blind or visually-impaired players are assisted as appropriate. If wheelchair users are participating in a session, ensure all gangways and exits are kept sufficiently clear of obstacles.

For further information, contact the National Equality and Child Protection Officer at the ETTA headquarters office or e-mail: judy.rogers@etta.co.uk

A wheelchair player executes a backhand push return.

As a coach of any players, disabled or able-bodied, you should always ask the player if you are in doubt over some element of the player's health or capabilities.

A wheelchair player executes a backhand service.

Tactical advice is given to a player at the end of the first game.

ADMINISTRATION

Table tennis is administered at local, regional and national levels. At the top, is the International Table Tennis Federation (ITTF). Made up of member countries' national governing body associations, it is responsible for the game's rules.

ORGANISATION

The European Trade Tennis Union (ETTU) is responsible for competitive play in Europe whilst the English Table Tennis Association Ltd (ETTA) is the governing body of the sport in England. The English Schools Table Tennis Association (ESTTA) is an organisation backed by the ETTA, and is responsible for all school competitions. The British Table Tennis Association for People with Disabilities (BTTAD) is another organisation backed by the ETTA, and is responsible for all training and competitions that are specifically organised for disabled players. Further details of all these associations can be obtained from:

The General Secretary
English Table Tennis Association Ltd
Queensbury House
Havelock Road
Hastings
East Sussex
TN34 1HF

Tel: 01424 722525
Fax: 01424 422103
Email: admin@etta.co.uk
Website: www.etta.co.uk

COMPETITIVE PLAY

Many newcomers to table tennis begin by playing at a school, youth club or local table tennis club. As progress is made, competitive play is not only necessary to improve but also adds to the enjoyment of the game.

The English Schools Table Tennis Association (ESTTA) runs individual and team competitions for both boys and girls. These are open to any player who attends an affiliated school. The English Table Tennis Association (ETTA) is responsible for co-ordinating a programme of tournaments throughout the country for different age groups as follows:

- Cadet (under 15 years)
- Junior (under 18 years)
- Senior (over 18 years)
- Veteran (over 40 years)

These tournaments include singles and doubles events, and competitions defined by age group and ability level.

There are also British League competitions for junior, senior and veteran players. The above events are 'open' to all players who fulfil the competition's requirements. In addition, the table tennis calendar contains many 'closed' events, which are held with restrictions upon entries. For example, a 'Country Closed' tournament or competition is only for players who live in a particular area.

AFFILIATION

An affiliated player is one who attaches themselves to their national association, either directly or through membership of a club or affiliated organisation.
National governing bodies include:

The English Schools Table Tennis Association
36 Froom Street
Chorley
Lancashire
PR6 0AN

The Irish Table Tennis Association Ltd
46 Lorcan Villas
Santry
Dublin 9

The Scottish Table Tennis Association
Caledonia House
South Gyle
Edinburgh
EH12 9DQ

The Table Tennis Association of Wales
7 Hopkins Close
Thornbury
Bristol
BS35 2PX

GETTING NOTICED

Competition table tennis such as the events noted above all provide valuable match experience and help a talented player to be noticed by the selectors and perhaps be invited to join county, regional or national squad training camps.

Junior players competing at the European Youth Championships.

ALL-TIME GREATS

MEN

Victor Barna
Born Hungary, 24 August 1911
The greatest table tennis player of his generation, he created a record of performance that is unlikely ever to be equalled. In World Championships alone his personal achievement was fifteen individual titles plus seven gold medals as a member of winning Hungarian Swaythling Cup teams. He won five men's singles (four in a row), eight men's doubles and two mixed doubles.

Richard Bergmann
Born Austria, 10 April 1919
Perhaps the most purposeful and resolute fighter that table tennis has ever known. He never knew the meaning of defeat and against all types of opponents, and sometimes even the clock, he won four world singles titles. When only sixteen he was the key figure of the only Austrian team ever to win the Swaythling Cup and seventeen years later he helped England to win it.

Chuang Tse-tung
Born China, 1942
Chuang Tse-tung won the men's singles crown in three successive Championships, 1961, 1963 and 1965 and was considered by many to have been the complete hitting machine. Unlike most other penholders he had an attacking backhand to complement his forehand that sped like a bullet. His three finals against the hardly less remarkable Li Fu-jung were in the classical mould, acrobatic and breathtaking.

Jan-Ove Waldner
Born Sweden, 30 October 1965
Losing finalist in New Dehli 1987, Jan Ove Waldner proved conclusively, that he had lost none of his outstanding skills by taking the crown in Dortmund, Germany, 1989. He became the first shakehands player to win the singles title for six years. Sweden has produced many fine players in recent years and Waldner has been the star with his all round game and amazing reflexes.

WOMEN

Ruth Aarons
Born USA, 1919
The only American to win a singles title and the youngest player ever to do so. In 1936, aged 16 years and nine months, she won the title by a combination of brilliant defence and athleticism. In 1937 she was involved in the only disqualification of both players in a final, and as a protest at the decision, announced her immediate retirement.

Angelica Rozeanu
Born Romania, 15 October 1921
Made sporting history on two counts, as she became the first Romanian woman to win a world title in any sport, and then surpassed the proud record of Maria Mednyanszky, by winning the women's singles title on six consecutive years. As the World Championships are now held biennially, it is unlikely that this record will ever be equalled, let alone beaten.

The Rowe Twins
Born England, 14 April 1933
Rosalind and Diane were World Doubles Champions in 1951 and 1954. These two delightful teenagers won the title at their first attempt. They went on to reach the final of the women's doubles for five consecutive years, winning twice, the second time on the night of their 21st birthday. The Rowe Twins were famous throughout the world, appearing on the front of newspapers and even playing an exhibition in Sweden's Royal Palace with Prince Gustav as their ball boy!

GLOSSARY

Attacker A player who uses mainly topspin strokes to win a point.

Backspin When the ball is rotated anticlockwise by brushing the ball at the bottom.

Bat Proper name is the racket, which is used to strike the ball.

Blade Flat part of the racket, used to strike the ball; often made of wood, and provides the surface for the rubber and sponge to be attached.

Defender A player who plays defensively, using mainly backspin strokes to win a point.

Doubles A game of table tennis played between two pairs of players, with players on each side taking it in turns to hit the ball.

Free hand The hand not holding the racket.

Game A set amount of play. The first player to reach 11 points wins, unless both players have 10 points. In this case, the game is won by the player who manages to get a lead of 2 points.

Grip The method a player uses to hold the racket. The main grips are 'shake-hands' and 'penhold'.

Let Describes a rally that is not completed, meaning that no score is recorded for either player.

Lob An advanced topspin stroke. The lob is played well back from the table, and is struck high and long on to the opponent's side of the table.

Loop An attacking topspin stroke, played close to the table.

Match Consists of an odd number of games (see above) e.g. 3, 5 or 7.

Net An obstacle 15.25cm (6 in) high strung across the middle of the table, over which the ball is played.

Point A service or rally after which a point is scored by the winner.

Practice When a rally or rallies are played in order to improve technique but without points being scored.

Racket hand The hand carrying or holding the racket.

Ready stance The position a player takes up at the table in readiness to play, alert and with the feet slightly apart for good balance.

Receiver The player who receives the ball after it has been served, i.e. strikes the ball second in a rally.

Server The player who serves the ball, i.e. strikes the ball first in a rally.

Rubber Material used to cover the blade, which often has sponge underneath it.

Sidespin When the ball is rotated left or right by brushing the ball sideways when hitting it with the racket.

Singles A game of table tennis played between two players.

Sponge Soft, springy material found between the rubber and blade on most rackets.

Stroke Describes the technique and style with which the ball is struck.

Table An elevated playing surface that is 2.74m (9 ft) long, 1.525m (5 ft) wide and 76cm (2 ft 6 in) above the floor.

Topspin When the ball is rotated anticlockwise by brushing it at the top when it is hit with the racket.

TABLE TENNIS CHRONOLOGY

1880s Adaption of lawn tennis to the dining table, using improvised equipment.

1890s Several patents registered in England. Manufactured sets produced under trade names such as Gossima, Ping Pong and Whiff-Waff and sold with simple rules.

1900 Development of celluloid balls to replace rubber and cork ones.

1900–1905 Table tennis becomes a popular game in the Western world.

1901 Table Tennis Association and rival Ping Pong Association formed in England. First books on the game published in England.

1902 Table Tennis and Pastimes Pioneer published. A set of twelve picture postcards on the game were printed.

1902–03 Mr E. C. Goode of Putney, London, becomes the first player to win a major tournament using a racket covered with pimpled rubber.

1903 Amalgamation of the Table Tennis Association and the Ping Pong Association.

1905 In England the game fades into obscurity but is continued in several European countries.

1922 Revival of the game in England and establishment of standard Laws. A mammoth tournament is organised by the *Daily Mirror*, which attracts 40,000 entrants.

1923 The Welsh Association is formed. In China the Shanghai Ping Pong Union is inaugurated.

1926 The International Table Tennis Federation (ITTF) is initiated in Berlin. The First World Championships is held in London. The Swaythling Cup is inaugurated.

1936 The Tenth World Championships is held in Prague. The longest rally takes place, the first point taking over 2 hours.

1937 To encourage attacking play rule changes are brought in, with the net lowered to 15.25cm (6 in), and a time limit of 20 minutes per game and finger spin prohibited.

1952 The Nineteenth World Championships is held in Bombay, India – the first to be staged in Asia – marking Japan's entry to the international scene. Hiroji Satch of Japan becomes the first player to win a world championship using a racket covered in thick sponge.

1959 Rackets are standardised, with the elimination of thick sponge.

1967 European League competition begins.

1969 Richard Bergmann, four times World Singles Champion dies aged 50.

1971 First Commonwealth Championships held in Singapore. Western teams invited to tour China. Afro-Asian Tournament held in Peking, with 700 competitors.

1972 Victor Barna, winner of fifteen individual gold medals in the World Championships, dies in Lima, Peru. Experimentation with yellow balls.

1977 The ITTF receive formal declaration of their recognition by the International Olympic Committee (IOC).

1978 Norwich Union Grand Prix inaugurated. Maria Mednyanszky, winner of eighteen individual World titles, dies in Budapest, Hungary, aged 77.

1979 First European World Championships for Paraplegics held in Stoke Mandeville, England.

1980 Ruth Aarons, the youngest ever winner of the World Women's Singles Championship, dies in the USA.

1982 First World Veterans' Championships held in Gothenberg, Sweden. First World Championships for Paraplegics held in Stoke Mandeville, England.

1983 Racket to have different colours on its two faces, and ban put on 'foot stamping' during service.

1985 First ever confrontation of top players from Europe and Asia held in Rome. Racket coverings restricted to black and bright red, and the prize money limit is removed.

1988 Table tennis is featured for the first time in the Olympic Games in Seoul, South Korea.

1990 Bohumil Vana, winner of four individual gold medals in World Championships, dies in his country of birth, Czechoslovakia.

1992 Former World Champion Jan-Ove Waldner becomes Olympic singles champion, and reputedly, the first table tennis millionaire.

INDEX